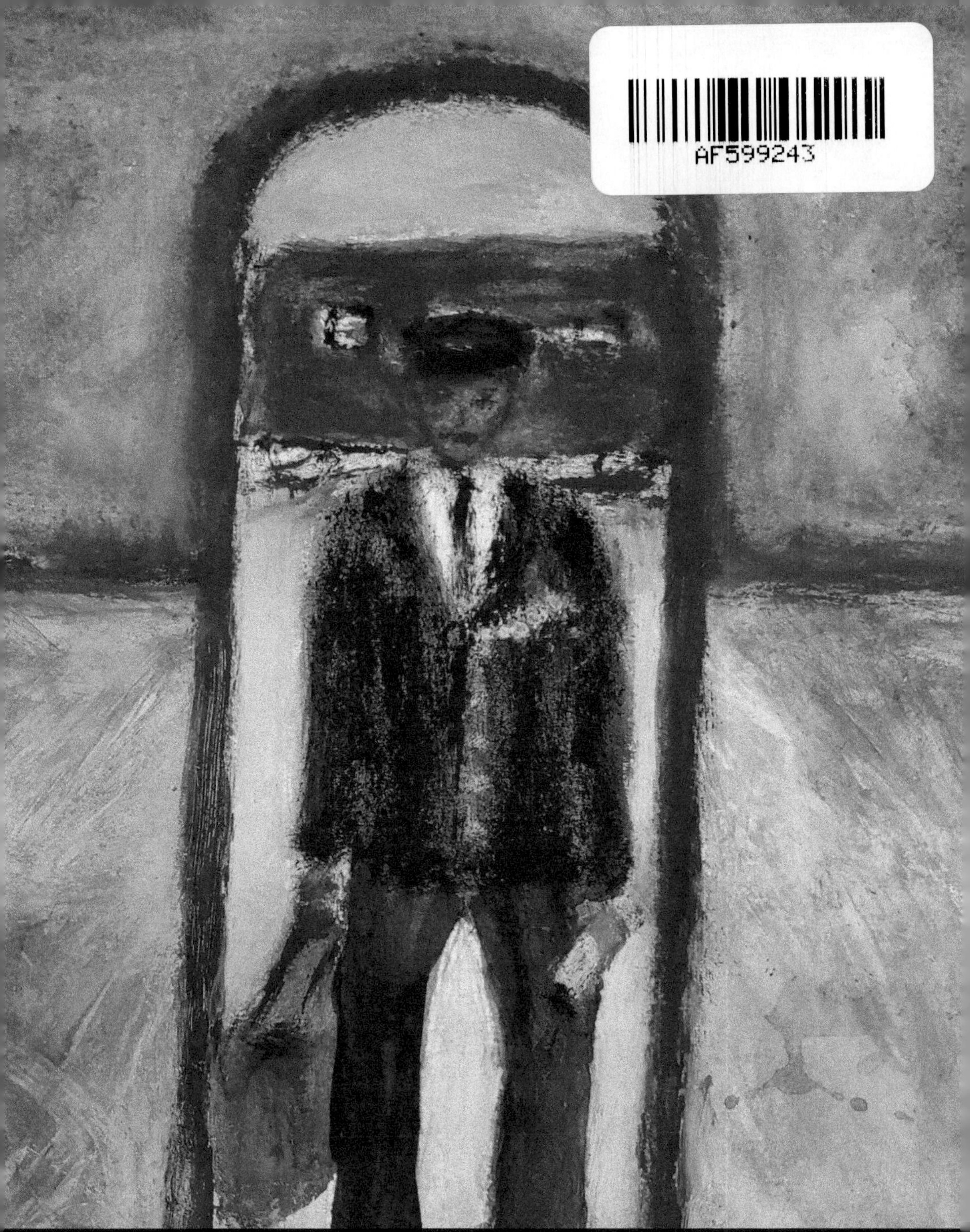

MERVYN TAYLOR

GETTING THROUGH

MERVYN TAYLOR

GETTING THROUGH

NEW & SELECTED POEMS

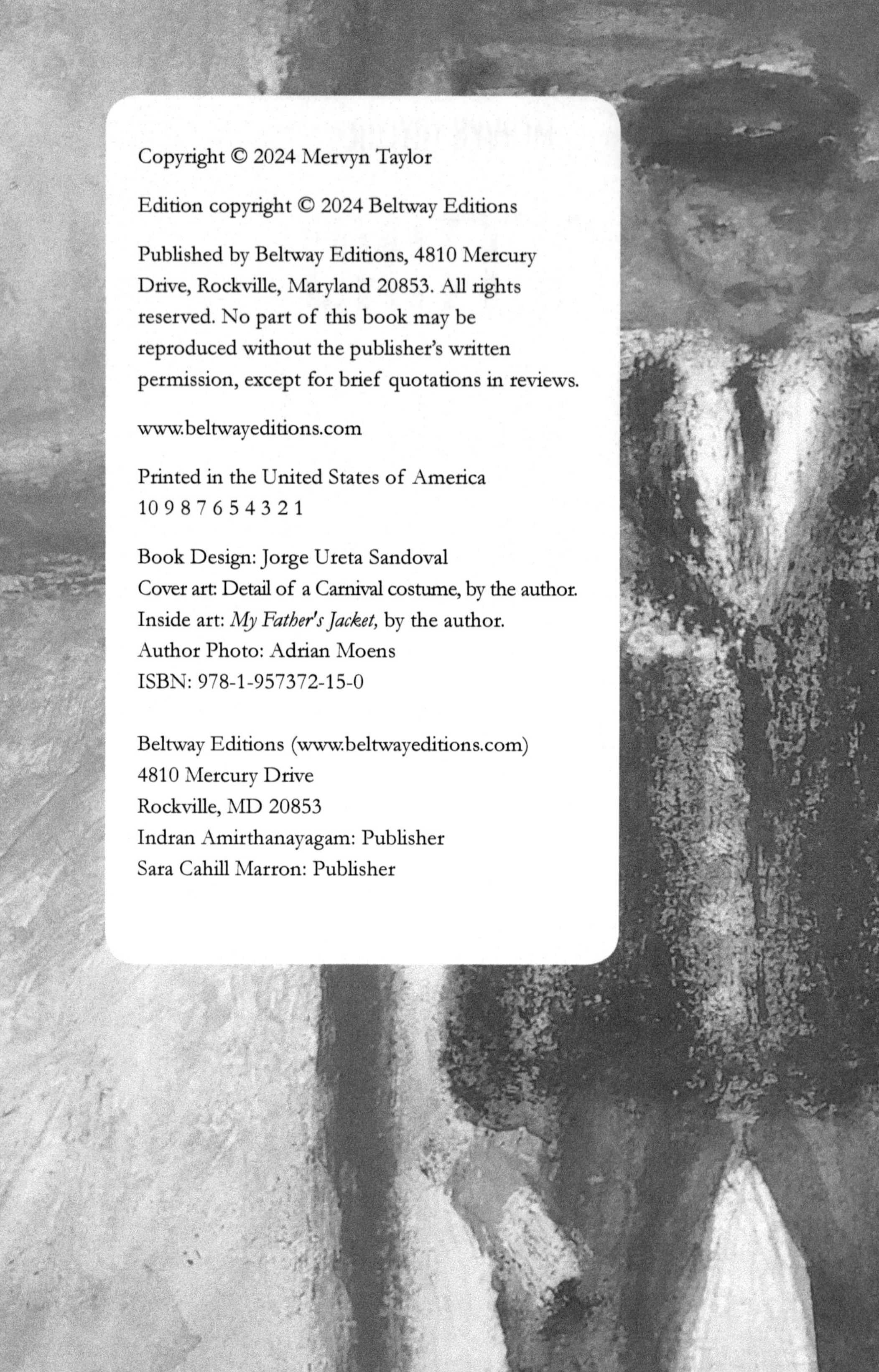

Published by Beltway Editions, 4810 Mercury Drive, Rockville, Maryland 20853.

www.beltwayeditions.com

Printed in the United States of America
10 9 8 7 6 5 4 3 2 1

Book Design: Jorge Ureta Sandoval
Cover art: Detail of a Carnival costume, by the author.
Inside art: *My Father's Jacket,* by the author.
Author Photo: Adrian Moens
ISBN: 978-1-957372-15-0

Beltway Editions (www.beltwayeditions.com)
4810 Mercury Drive
Rockville, MD 20853
Indran Amirthanayagam: Publisher
Sara Cahill Marron: Publisher

FOR MY GRANDCHILDREN

CONTENTS

No Back Door (2010)

The Waving Gallery (2014)

Voices Carry (2017)

Country of Warm Snow (2020)

News of the Living (2020)

The Last Train (2023)

I MAKE A SCIENCE OF EVERYTHING—
THE ORANGE RIND DRYING IN THE
KITCHEN, THE DOGGISH WAY
THE MOON HERDS THE STARS …

FROM “THE OUTING”

Solace

It rained all night. I took
comfort in that—the space
between stars, the dark
wound of the sky.

The earth, and all her
inhabitants stood under
some broadleaf plant,
water dripping onto

our backs. And if
there were places
where the sun shined
on playful bodies, we

weren't aware. Only
of bombs disguised
as rain, till the last
minute when they

hit, and then, as
someone sang long ago,
it seemed it was raining
all over the world.

Send This to the Poets

For they are finding it
impossible these days
to delight anyone with what
they can muster from the pool
collecting at their feet
of dead letters fallen
like feathers from molting birds

There is a war in the mountains
and another in the desert and
a tumult of refugee boats
and storied cruise ships
floundering among rogue waves
an audience of whales gathered
at the surface and blowing

Send this to the poets on farms
pretending they know how to work
the milking machines
and to the ones digging in the rubble
of bombed-out cities and
running to hospitals
blown up as they run

Send it on the smallest slips of paper
undetectable in the many searches
to be endured at this checkpoint
send it to those whose job is to find
in this stadium of stanzas
some rhyme or reason
why they should exist at all

A Rescue in Gaza

It always rains the night before
my birthday, when I wait to see
who will call first, my daughter

or my son. In the morning it's
still raining, and I haven't heard
from either one. On Facebook,

I read birthday greetings, but
my eyes are drawn to the picture
of a child lifted from the rubble,

mud caking both eyes. And I
make a wish that his rescuers
return him whole to his family,

who cannot bear to hear any
more poems of love and death,
walking together like good friends.

The Strip

Back in Trinidad, we had our own
Gaza, a stretch of road where rum
flowed, and tempers flared all night.

It ran alongside the sea that sighed
as women hid knives in their bras and
lied to the police. In time, our Strip

faded, only remembered now that
bombs are dropping on the real Gaza
on the other side of the world, where

veils are lifted to identify little girls
as tanks rumble through streets, and
the sea runs away from the shore.

When the Dance Floor Collapsed

There was a big wedding
in the Middle East, more than
a hundred guests circling the
happy couple, the band playing,

the dancers clapping, when
the floor gave way, and
the crowd disappeared in a
sea of taffeta and blended wool.

The cymbals crashed, the piano
lost its keys, the horns grew
silent. Guests who had been
seated around the perimeter

gazed into the abyss, stunned.
Today, that building is gone,
a pile of rubble like all the rest,
bombs having flattened the city.

And the couple think of their
wedding day, of shattered glass
and the singer's voice, faint
but distinct, calling for help.

Life of Refugees

So they must move again,
to a place nearer the sea,
where ships go about their

nefarious business. There's
no Cape of Good Hope, only
bandy-legged men swearing

they know another way. *Leave*
it, the wife tells the husband,
we have no place to put it

where we are going. And
where is that blessed corner,
where our house will not

blow up, the boat not capsize,
the guard not ask for papers,
our children not appear in rags,

running across a landscape
in which we've become so
familiar, wolves lick our hands.

Death of Poets

You hope their magical lines
will save them, keep them
like kites in the Savannah,

never to go sailing over
Queen's Royal College,
tangled in one of those tall

trees with awkward limbs.
You believe they must have
one more chance at perfect

rhyme, a metaphor so stunning
it climbs out of what surely
looked like ruin, like coffin

kites flouncing in the strong
wind, riding the gust with
tails made from bedding.

Ah, Derek, ah, Lucille!
Your followers run through
deserted streets where we

think you might've gone
down, pitched like stars, only
to find you taken back up,

invisible, the thread bellying
and sawing, which is how
we know you're still there.

On Not Hearing from Someone

for S. C.

Used to be the business of life
had swept them along, currents
as playful as those of the Ulanga

River, in *The African Queen.*
But this is no movie—a voice
from your days suspiciously

absent, a whole piano missing,
cartoon legs in the air. And so
you dig, hoping to hear news of

the best sort, that your friend's
on the coast somewhere, playing
one of those crazy clubs, or just

mad about something you did,
knowing how dizzy you can be,
calling her by her dead sister's name.

Pause

They say that Miles, at one
point in his career, forgot
how to play. Once,

in Central Park, we held
our breath while he took
so long between notes,

we were afraid something
terrible had happened. But
then the clearest sound

broke the silence, and if
he'd walked off, we'd
have followed him into

the reservoir. So he
must have been practicing
leaving that space,

that interlude where
the cleft untangles itself
from the rest of the world,

forgetting to call us
across the universe,
Here, Faithful, here.

Soft Shoe

I remember the time
Sammy Davis Jr. came
to the Globe and Uncle Syl

took us to see him tap dance
and draw his six shooters
at lightning speed.

Sammy had recently
lost an eye. I'd read
about how it happened,

when a woman backed
into his lane somewhere
in Florida, his face hitting

the bullet-shaped horn.
I almost cried when he sang
"Mr. Bojangles." And when

he did the old soft shoe, I
shuffled my feet under my seat,
keeping one eye closed.

Listening to Nancy Wilson

We were in the kitchen
listening to her sing
"The Very Thought of You"

when a jealous girlfriend
burst in and slammed
the arm off the record.

We sat there as she headed
out the door, player under
one arm, books under the other.

Years later, news of Nancy's
passing would remind me of that
morning, the screech of the needle.

Cataract

A plane blinks its way
between the blades of the fan
in my window, headed north
in the dark. On tonight's news,

they showed an aircraft's nose,
smashed by a flock of birds,
a woman in a window seat saying
one wing looked ready to fall off.

I lay here thinking about the
passengers who just flew over,
how safe they must feel the closer
they get to the airport. How reassuring,

that after surgery, the eye can
track an object thousands of feet
up, and come back to earth, find fireflies
flickering among trees in the park.

I Hear a Shout

And have no idea what it
is this time, the crazy guy
talking to his dogs again, a
victory for the ex-president?

But looking out, all appears
calm, the bag of trash waits
for pickup, the sun has climbed
a little higher, the Savannah

still the same sleepy green.
It must have been the voice
in my head, the one seeking
to raise an alarm over every

misunderstanding, every
body washed overboard in an
unfamiliar crossing, the train
I hear leaving for the camps,

the dumbness of not knowing
which way it's headed this
time, the cock crow sounding
almost human, *Derail, derail!*

The Stubborn Sea

Returns to see what we've made of
the land after all these years, if we've
built more than cages, and plastic flotillas.

If we've managed to cause fewer refugee
camps, tent cities, those signs
of dismal failure.

Prayers we have aplenty, nailed
to the foot of every cross, a vision of
another planet called heaven, where

we've stocked the shelves with all the
goods we have a taste for, the songs
we know to sing. But that one

we'll despoil soon enough,
this earth made smaller and smaller,
in the whittler's hands.

Stickfight

Carnival Monday, Skinny was always the first to get his head split. We would sight him, barefoot as usual, headband tied tight, brandishing his bois, striding confidently towards Tiger Cat Bar, where the drums were beating loudly. Some young fighter would be prancing there, assured of at least one victory that morning.

Skinny's friend Shadow would walk to meet him, to give him some word of counsel, to which Skinny would pay no heed. Without breaking stride, he would brush Shadow aside, eyes red and purposeful from the two shots of puncheon he'd had before setting out.

A short titter of laughter ran through the crowd gathered outside the bar. Skinny would challenge his opponent, pointing his stick and caraying, as they say. It didn't last long. Three minutes of circling and parrying and whap! The kerchief on Skinny's head turned a quick red, the young fighter giving a jubilant yell, his friends cheering as the chantwells escorted the injured man to the pavement across the road, out of the sun.

To his credit, Skinny never made a sound after being hit, not a moan, not a cry. After a few minutes of ministration from the women, he would rise, shoulder his stick and walk silently back the way he'd come. The next time they'd see him would be Carnival Tuesday, when dressed as a standard bearer in Big Wilfred's portrayal of "Feast of Belshazzar," he would wear a feathered helmet that covered his bandaged head, and sandals strapped up to the knees, that being the one day of the year he wore shoes.

Mas

In the Roman band, Valmon played
Nero, cape covering the intersection
of Jerningham and Norfolk, his wife

with four great spotted dogs not far
behind, as if both these characters
had climbed down from the screen

at Olympic and landed here, on
Carnival Day, to have us till today
recalling and talking and forgiving

him for cheating us out of our money,
promising to bring Sam Cooke to
Trinidad, so even when we spotted

the thief on Frederick Street years
later, wanting to cuff him down, we
said instead, *Nero, boy, that was mas.*

Characters

for Michael Anthony (1932-2023)

In "The Year in San Fernando,"
the boy from Mayaro sent
to stay with relatives

won't eat till the others are done.
The one in "The Games Were Coming"
slips out in his mother's dress

to find the J'ouvert with its darkness
and strange, scary masquerade.
There's the hedge through which

he slips back in, so the house
would never know he'd left,
the sun coming up on the man

with two first names,
as if to keep him young
all his days, hearing the sea.

Learning to Walk All Over Again

for JB

Once a waiter on Amtrak, he now
has trouble walking on solid ground,
feet trying to grip the floor as when
the train sped through the Rockies.

He has a hard time going up a hill
in Northwest D.C. for a rehab
meeting, the concrete underfoot
not swaying or giving an inch.

Learning to walk again, he uses
his pet phrase—*tall, bald, and that*
ain't all—and a stick from the smooth
birch growing outside his window.

Evening

When the light stays close
to the earth, when you can
touch it, like paper, make

a kite and fly it over houses
and cemeteries and grass
on the green Savannah,

when it lasts
long enough to let your
sadness sail like a ship

with four masts and
doubtful cargo, your
dreams below deck,

the waterline taking its
measure from your tears,
the twilight will allow

this time for your moping.
Then it's back to rehearsal,
landlocked beings

that we are: kite flyers,
dancers on the shore,
praying the hour lasts long.

Cafe on the Old Airport Road

When I ask what's for breakfast,
the proprietress smiles and says, *liver.*

She's been here a long time, long before
they built the new airport, and the

Customs Office, which opens at eight.
I marvel at her beautiful name, Sintra.

On every table, there's a vase of wildflowers.
She laughs at my offer to help run this place.

So what did you try to smuggle in, she asks.
And howls when I answer, *peanuts.*

Creatures

There are at least fifty turtles sunning
on a rock, near where the lake curves
like a palette around a painter's thumb.

At the foot of the bridge there are more,
crowded onto smaller stones, jostling
each other for space, the littler ones

falling back, shells glistening as they
try again to find a footing. Such a
pastime I imagine must be fun, here

and there a cracked shell saying,
Not always, not always. Some end up
on their backs, waiting to be nudged.

I met a woman one day, standing guard
over a baby turtle that had strayed some
distance from the water, a poet who'd

written such a story of hurt and recovery,
looking into her eyes was hard. I left her
scanning the reeds for one of the workers

with green badges, who would know
how to carry the animal to a safe place.
On the far side of the lake is a gaggle

of geese, cavorting and minding their
own. Ah, the honking noise they
make, amid the silence of others.

Petticoat Princess

for Sabina Chebichi

Wearing only a bright green petticoat,
she runs barefoot, ahead of the others
in their fancy sneakers and shorts

with stripes down the sides. At home,
her mother sits by the radio yelling,
go, go, outside the whole village

shouting itself hoarse. The bell
rings as she takes the last turn,
petticoat flying around her dark legs,

toes coated with dust. The sponsors
cannot wait for her to wear their
shoes, the ones with the *swoosh*.

The Blind Storyteller

carries his invalid friend
up and down the city streets.

While he tells stories, his friend
sells sweets, and listens attentively,

though he's heard most of the tales
many times before. After he dies,

the storyteller will grieve for days,
missing the weight on his back,

unsure then of his stories, who will
clap so long and happily in his ear.

New Days

And we are glad for the air
cooled after last night's storm,
the confused dream sorted out.

Some new industry starts today,
the sign out front changed, the
former owner gone back to

Minnesota, the Quaker school
he attended still on the corner.
What do new days have to do

with the one we lived yesterday?
Nothing. Paint and the spelling
of a company name changed.

Old men sit in rockers or
wheelchairs, vines choking
the blooming frangipani—

This is where I used to park
my bike, there beneath
the Treasury's marble stairs.

That's the window where we
spied the clerk leaving early to
catch his bus. Only new days

return the light of the stars.
Picture a man, parents buried
under a spruce on his farm,

wondering where the swallows
went after he left, that winter
when the snow refused to fall.

Shorten the Chain

It's how you control the dog,
so he doesn't control you.
So says the homeless man

who has made camp
in the middle of the Savannah
with his wild pack,

who waves me away, yelling,
Shorten the chain!
Which works to this day.

On Hearing My Uncle Use Profanity for the First Time

It was a Saturday, the day I usually went by to see if I might get some movie money. I stood at the upstairs entrance to my uncle's club with an employee who told me to wait.

Through the half-open door, I heard the clink of glasses and watched Uncle Syl shoot pool, going around the table in the most casual but purposeful manner, telling his opponent that he was "too fucking stupid."

I'd never heard him curse before. The guy standing there with me glanced down, to see if I'd heard. He ran to my uncle, who looked up, seeing me there for the first time.

I remained in the doorway, witnessing a strange tableau: the player on the opposite side of the table staring, the man whispering in my uncle's ear, my uncle holding his cue like a weapon, his hat slanted at an angle I never noticed before.

An Essay Almost Ruined by Nightmarish Punctuation

after Joseph Brodsky

Like our lives, I suppose, stopping
when we should be going, pausing
to have a war or two, then rambling

on about death and shadows, a
plethora of commas marking our
progress, like crosses along the

Appian Way. And so we go, from
pillar to post, shoveling a new road
feet from where we stand, praying

the bridge, whose name we change
in crossing, holds up. Meanwhile
the tall edifice we erected waits

to fall, the exclamation that means
we're lost, and need a moment
to get our bearings, to decide

if to turn back, or to proceed,
those behind following blindly,
trusting an idea up ahead.

The Patient

for Fifi

In the ICU at the hospital,
I sit like a kid on punishment
in a corner of your room.

Your son glances at me as he
tries to convince you that you'd
be fine, once the new liver kicks in.

You smile at one of the orderlies
who resembles a boy from your village
who thought you so pretty.

Embarrassed, your boy gets up
to leave as the doctor,
thinking me family,

describes the procedure they hope
to begin. I'm the boyfriend
no one knew existed.

After they pull the plug, it's
thirty minutes before I die, you
whispered when I first came in.

Center of the World II

1.

I look again from the window,
and there's the V-shaped light of
the Mexican food truck, beyond it

the ghostly green of the subway
doors, late workers stopping
in front of the supermarket to read

posters for tomorrow's bargains.
The noonday drinkers have left one
Styrofoam cup on a sidewalk table,

hands stretched to reach it, voices
shrill in the air, though they're no
longer there. I wonder who takes

them in for the night, who listens
to the number they swear will win,
the exact total of antlers on the herd

in their recurring dreams, nightly
stampeded by wolves—twenty-two,
they repeat, they counted twenty-two.

2.

At this late hour, a young girl enters
the park for her run, disappearing
under the branches that hide the lake,

now that it's summer. I see the lights
of scooters that explode in hallways,
dodging in and out of shadow. Poor

girl has no idea she's in for the run
of her life. *C'dere*, as my old Bajan
landlord used to say, *Blouse and skirt.*

3.

The 4th has come and gone, gunfire
and fireworks indistinguishable, the
man dousing people with fire mousey

before the cameras. *He has no owner,*
my mother would affirm, his victims
trees without leaves. I have lived here

more than forty years now, from Latin
to Calypso and back again, crack in
the interim, the Drummer's Grove

embroidered with strands of blue
smoke from weed and barbecue. I
used to make the full circle, now

the hill is a challenge. I cut through
the part where the guys with their
fancy rods fish and throw back,

their world different from the rest,
the domino players, the shy turtles
grouped on rocks, a crowd of shells.

4.

My phone rings: someone wants to
know if it's true, a friend returned
to the island has died? No, I spoke

with him last night, the murderous
count hasn't reached him yet. Here
in Brooklyn, when Labor Day comes,

they miss his J'ouvert band, his crazy
antics, the Kente Kingdom he closed
with. His wish? For his ashes, when

the time arrives, to be spread in the
Savannah, where horses' hooves left
a trail for him to find the way home.

Getting Through?

This is the question they ask
in the dry goods store as I
go down a crowded aisle.

Did you try Nagib? They have
the headless nails. What I
need, Miss, I believe sold out

long ago—the smile on Marcia
Sampson's face, the dimple
in Patsy Sombrano's cheek.

All these years away, no one
thought to ask. But in a country
with roads that end at the sea

and up in the hills, it's easy to spot
a soul at the grassy edge, who
should've gotten through, by now.

~AN ISLAND OF HIS OWN~

(1992)

On Sundays Like This

On Sundays like this, I can't sleep.
A friend from Miami comes to show me
what made her stepfather lust when
she was younger. I long to call someone
and say, I'm sick from last night.
I keep going from the bed to the door,
thinking the poetry at the coffee house
is good, and could console my friend.
I turn to a picture of my father,
taken just as he had given in,
and I tell my friend from Florida, no,
men are not always hungry. Sometimes
they starve, after some terribly long night,
sometimes, on Sundays like this,
they civilize themselves to stone.

The Conductor

His cap in curling letters said, *Guard.*
He left early in the morning, and
as soon as he came home, he polished
his buttons with a U-shaped thing.
He didn't have many friends.

I remember only Telemaque, who
brought provisions and cane and wore
khaki with great stains at the armpits,
who laughed when my father teased him
about how short his wife's hair was,
how his house was so small.

My father's train went east, to Sangre Grande.
All the way there I dozed, waking to feel
his serge sleeve against my cheek, his
grown-up breath in the fabric as he pointed out
his friend Telemaque's house, and it was small.

At the depot in Sangre Grande, there was
a woman, surprised when she saw me
under the mosquito netting. After she left,
my father filled notebooks with numbers,
his pen scratching away in the silence
as now and then he glanced out the window
towards the other side of the tracks
where the green fields began.

The Wall

One of the great joys then was running
out past The Neck into that hard ground
called The Test where low prickly briars
grew all over except on the narrow trail
that shot off the left of the highway
and zigzagged crazily between the cars
and the sea, along which a boy was trampled
who had stopped to pee or look at a mouse
or something in the underbrush.
At all hours they would be out there,
at night in fluorescent shorts in the fog
they would pace the cars, breathing
like small separate engines, and sometimes
in the headlights near the last exit
one would appear, breathless and begging
for a ride as far as the bridge. There was
a small red warning sign near the slipway
where in the war days ships were repaired,
where someone had run right over
the wall, and had been heard by the others,
drowning in the dark. There were guys
in dented pickup trucks who slept
in their cabs on the rim of the road and
waited for the runners to come, who would
call them *sick fucks*, and by the numbers
on their sweaters. So they began to run
with knives in their socks, and whistles
round their necks, and to crouch low
without breaking speed. In winter

the ice would make one slip sometimes,
and he would go for yards into the brush,
the cuts deepening the red of his face,
the others rushing past, looking only
at the distance stretching ahead. It was
far from houses where they went, and
no one knew where, or if that track
had an end. But the seagulls streamed
in that direction, becoming specks
before flying back, grazing the
shoulders of that statue in the sea.

Ode to Retirement

for Pat Ralphs

So you've gone queer
and quit your job
to run a gondola ferry
in Venice.

Or did you decide
on the Cameroons,
that moonstruck beach
meant to be included
in memoirs?

Or is it the antique trade,
after all. So many choices.
But as you ride
the Orient Express, a good
gentleman at your service,

how bad can it be?
You can paint your place
any color you want and
stop and wonder whatever
happened to the Mays boys.

And when it's been
a rough day at the shop
you can pack up,
pull on the old straw
and without a word
to anyone, go home.

Mixed Blessings

At the funeral, they asked McNeill
to eulogize his aunt. After all, he
was the poet in the family.
And when he said unbecoming things,
they were shocked, unable
to hide their discomfort.

And the Anglican priest, and
the acolyte boy allergic to flowers,
waited. And the old caretaker
down by the gate jingled his keys,
and the woman in white who
had led the procession wailed
while blossoms of frangipani
fell on them. Still, McNeill

droned on in that voice of his,
about his aunt's madness and decline,
while her casket sat upon the brink,
the glass oval grown cloudy,
as if she had resumed breathing.
And the men with shovels clinked,
lit up, and smoked again.

Then, when the canon's signal
finally caught his eye, McNeill
read one last verse, about
there being no end to wickedness,

and closed the book, nearly tripping
on one of the lowering ropes, as
someone shouted, *Amen!*
and they let her down, quickly.

An Island of His Own

In his new kingdom, he conquered
the conditions of exile. He scaled
the high cliffs to prolong the sunset,
and learned to relish the reward
of a desolate day. He'd sit on
the rocks and write to no one
in particular that the gulls were
consistent in the pattern of their
flight, as he became more and more
obstinate about not changing
his clothes, letting the sun
dry them on his back when
he came out of the sea.

If he missed anything, it was
breaking the old laws and
observing the tantrums of women
when he stood their daughters
against the old cannon. Which
explains the tonnage of his guilt
and why he scratched to bleeding
his tenderest parts. But out here,
there's only the wind to contend
with. The ground under his hut
undulated, so he slid into the
cornices, and avoided boredom.

He would fix the old lacework
till it was beyond repair and
then recite something he wrote

yesterday, or ten years ago, when
there were green and overflowing
images of rivers called Orinoco
in his poems. He'd call them all
my old friends, and hooking his arm
like a woman, would lead off
thus accompanied, into
another song about the sea.

The Man Who Never Saw the Sea

Out there is an ancient fish,
a giant moray that invites
the world to dinner.

Inland are mountains and
a man who loves his privacy.

Each is lucky to know exactly
what song the other
is singing, who's

calling you, *ooh, ooh, ooh.*

But the man has never
seen the sea. Not once
has ever been to the shore.

Shopping

Spotting the lady in the parlor
speaking confidentially
to the shopkeeper,

I'd come and stand behind her
before taking my hand
and hefting the plaid

where one buttock outweighed
the other. And as she spun and
chided, half adult, half child,

the bees went wild
above the sugar bags, while
old Aleong kept his head down

over the tureen, measuring
four cents' worth of
the good salt butter.

The Outing

And when there is
no more ice in the cooler,
and the kids hang
their heads out the car,
I turn to her and say,
Drive.

We don't honey
each other, we sit
silent in the sunset.
Out over the hood
the taillights swarm, I'm
in the mood for darkness
and jazz.

Sitting, we travel
like a drawing room
that moves. One kid
holds a shell he eased
out of the sand. It's
all the money we have,

saved for coziness
and sex, and sidelong
looks at the sea.
The sea? Yes, I make
a science of everything—

the orange rind
drying in the kitchen,

the doggish way the moon
herds the stars. Were it not
for the road under us,
we'd slip into the fields.
Faster, I say.

Woman on the Q

She could show you pictures
of her youngest, gone to stay
with grandfather in the bad time,

if she had the trunk for this key.
Or these yellow pearls, see
these? They broke and rolled

all over the *Belle Rose* floor.
She could show you the dance
that was doing then. You

wouldn't remember Phips, he
was her partner. You wouldn't
remember when her stockings

matched and stayed up without
knotting. See how things always
undo, always unravel? If only

she had the trunk on this train,
imagine how much more
she could show you.

Lady of the Lost

She goes away, but always returns,
just when I'm turning around, near
panic, ready to run, she shows me
a tree, and I remember this place:
the fiber floor stretching for more
than a mile under the coconut,
the grasscutter's sickle rising
and falling in a green shower,
the bathers changing behind
the bushes on the open beach.

But she doesn't stay. When I'm
halfway across the bridge buckling
over the second river, the lunar
monkey laughing *tee-hee*, the
black water sluggish and scary,
I see fire in the ferryhouse window,
where she's chatting and having tea.

O, love, she says, *you're so afraid
the city might sleep without you,
another hand undo the hours of
cornrowing*. She knows I'll fetch
the bucket, grumbling, that I'll
fret all night about this Manzanilla
moon, afraid to sleep under it,

while she goes wading the river,
the tar that bubbles on this island.
No buses come this far; I hear

only children on dark verandas
learning things by heart, the
punishing swish of the trees.
I call her every name under the
hissing gas of lamps in houses
so far apart, they are stars, and
she’s the one gone out among them.

~THE GOAT~

(1999)

On the Ave

It's one of those nights
when the intersection is crazy
with cars, the park pavilion's
a sea of crack vials,
and the lady downstairs
keeps calling the cops.
Should we go out from
our prison or just stay away
from the window? Perhaps
we might intercede
in someone's loneliness: *Hi!*
At least the phone's working.
Someone's dialing like mad
in the booth on the corner,
biting the end of a blue scarf
and turning her back to the world.
There's an ambulance
screaming up the avenue
for the guy spinning
in his wheelchair, the one
paramedics don gloves to handle.
There's a red moon
to go with his craziness
and a gun salute from a rooftop.
Can we be seen with the lights on?
Are they firing at the moon?

Back on Bergen

for Jay Kennedy

The lady on a corner stool
called for another drink,
the *No Credit* sign
flashing red in the window.

I was back on Bergen.
I thought I heard you
upstairs, where you lived
in the single apartment

so no one would hear
whenever you rehearsed,
or made love. Then
suddenly, the jukebox

came on, the singer
singing the same song
you sang that time
down at the Blue Coronet

when you caught
a frog in your throat
and a fan handed you
a glass of water

saying, *Take your time.*
You did, and
your voice returned,
ringing in the rafters.

Asylum

The week after the crab fest
at Stone Spring Asylum,
a patient in polka dots
picks shell from her hair.

She's waiting for a
cigarette break. In here,
everyone's a smoker. They
puff till their fingers burn.

The courtyard's a carpet
of filters. At a table,
a black man writes
a letter to his ex.

He shows it to his friend
who wears a helmet
to keep from banging
his head, who asks,

Why is it in red?

Soon everyone has
to have their medication.
As a door opens,
they form a line.

"O Baltimore, ain't it
hard to live?" It's Nina,
coming from earphones
someone left on a chair.

And spraying saliva
like a net, an inmate
with the disorder
called *perseverance*

begins with slow steps
measuring the distance
from this wall to that,
and from that wall to this.

The Mosque on Ninety-Sixth

Where the mosque sits now,
a Puerto Rican super once built
a summer residence to remind him
of home, a garden of statues and
chimes with a railed veranda,
a table for his boys to play cards on.

All that was missing was the sea.
In the summer, they could picture
it, but snow fell in December, and
company fell to Raphael, then none.
The super began to look like his
sculpted goats, stiff and white.

O, how our beards have grown,
they seemed to mutter, sounding
just like Raphael when he was
drunk and couldn't roll his r's.

The Lighthouse at Point Galera

You have to bend when you reach
the last landing, then you can straighten
as you step into the sunlight and look over
the rail, the sea spray reaching this high up,
the road going at an angle between the grass
and coconut palms, as if a child drew all this,
the isle of Tobago way out and gray, ashen
from lying in the water so long. The children
scream to hear how it echoes in the stairwell.
The keeper tells them they are too many,
but they climb anyway. He looks too young
to know the rocks, to warn a ship, or spot
a squall rising. Two boys sit near the turret
where the light flashes, and mimic the whistle
of local birds, everyone craning his neck,
unbelieving. It will be one hundred years
since they built this tower, and you can think
of many ways to commemorate the anniversary:
a coat of paint, a concert by the sea, an old salt
speaking in a recorded voice how, on such
and such a night, in the middle of his life,
he swam from the other island, the light
from Point Galera bringing him in. They
are all his offspring in these parts, too tired
as he was to move further inland. Or,
you can tell your own story, how you always
land by plane, and never saw this place
before, and that you believe the nun,
whose habit is in the trunk of her car,
that the great swimmer was her father.

Otto Holds the Fort

His addiction drove his family away.
Now he's older, and no longer draws
his blade at the slightest provocation,

although the temper that once led him
to smash a gambler's face with a lamp
still burns within. He's passionate

as ever about territory, and honor,
still has that grip which is at once
a welcome, and a warning.

When we meet, he offers the green,
green grass of home, the medicine
that can make sick dogs well again.

Green Tar

St. Margaret's Cemetery,
where Mr. Reid is buried,
is a mass of stone and tangle.

It's hard to think of him there,
whose pharmacy was pure order.
He'd fill each prescription with

close attention, holding the vials
up to the light, mouthing the daily
dosages—*once a day, twice a day.*

He'd parcel out his powders in
squares of pale paper, pestle barely
moving in the mortar. And they never

spoke of money, druggist or patient,
for times were tough, and medicine
like green tar hard enough to take.

A Few Words

for Rhona

The day he met her
talking to a boy on the bridge,
my father's question to my sister
was simple: *You studying*
man, or book?
And after he walked away,
the couple turned from each other,
the boy towards the Savannah,
my sister towards home.

~GONE AWAY~

(2006)

Agouti Look-Back

The Queen's Park Savannah
was always
one of the favorite places
to make out.

House of a Thousand Bedrooms,
we called it. Though it was dangerous,
and things could come crawling
through the grass, lovers
took their chances.

See them going, the man
with a rolled-up newspaper,
the woman walking ahead,
pretending not to be with him.

One morning, you might hear
a customer telling one of
the cooks at the Breakfast Shed
as she doubled with laughter,

about the old *agouti look-back*
that happened last night,
in that most public of places.

A Betting Man

When he can't be found at the office,
Harry's at the betting pool, picking Jetsam
in the second to win, and Crazy Ursula to place.

The top drawer of his desk overflows with
tickets. He's close to retirement, so whatever
he's been assigned goes to the new clerk.

In the parlor on Charlotte Street, where
there's always a card game going in the back,
he and his teacher friend scold each other

about bad habits. Harry picks his horses as
he does his friends, with blinders on. He
likes whom he likes, never bets on strangers.

Never mind who's riding Crazy Ursula,
Harry goes with her all the way.

Harry Goes Home

I hope the plane isn't crowded when
he goes, so he can stretch his legs
across three seats, and I hope that lady
I met when I traveled is working the
flight, so she will let him have as many
cushions as he wants and fix him
a meal of the soft stuff he only eats now,
and smile that pretty way of hers that
even his wife won't mind. And I hope

the pilot is one of those exceptional
BWee guys, who make it seem so easy
you hardly know when you land, just
a soft bump as you taxi in, who talk
the whole trip in the parlance Harry loves,
saying, instead of turbulence, *We just have
to make a little giddy in de hole*, so all
the passengers laugh, and feel comforted,
and raise their behinds and crane their
necks, so they can see each other.

And when they land, I want the sun to be
shining, or if it's drizzling, for a rainbow
to appear by the flyover, and his grandson
to be chatting incessantly all the way home
to his house in Turnback Alley, the breeze
laden with the heady scent of Ladies of
the Night, though it's only afternoon.

I want his wife and daughter to stand on
either side, their arms under his arms
so he can look past the rooftops down
to the sea, a steelband playing a familiar
tune, sunlight dancing on the waves, the
winter ache leaving his bones, a mischief
in his eyes as he glances at them both.

My Brother the Boxer

He likes to see
if I can take a punch,
folds his fist like a mallet
and hits me hard.

This is how he shows affection,
ready to spar
with one of my friends
as soon as I introduce them.

We are two sons
of a left-handed woman, one
wishing he had the killer jab,
the other encouraging,

poking at the
soft insides of his sibling,
feeling for the nerve
that *had* to be there.

Picture of a Man in a Rocker

After retiring from Princes Town Hospital,
Aunt Sheila looked after my father, working
her old needles, blunt as screws, into his arm.
I would sit watching, wincing as he winced.

When he died, having no pictures of him,
she sat him up in a rocker and had one taken.
Lifting him from the bed, she shunted him
off her hip, onto the cane-bottomed seat.

His feet brushed the carpet lightly before
she stooped, placing them on the crossbar. He
seemed to resist, grimacing the way he did
when anyone tried to kiss him. Except for

Cousin Judy, whom he let smooth his hair and
never bit, not even when she pried his lips open
to look at his teeth, which were all perfectly
straight and white till the day he passed.

As he sat upright in the rocker, I remember
how Sheila made the photographer wait, while
she adjusted my father's pajamas, and how,
in the snapshot, they had come undone again.

Prospect Park, September

Fall is a little ahead of itself this year, hurricanes
chasing each other out of the tropics. Winter's
coming, the storm when I'll stand at the window,
looking at the snow pile up. But for now,

the sun shines on the cyclists' helmets, and
a hawk hovers above the bike trail. Swans
cock their behinds in the air, and here come
the joggers, each with their own running style—

Olympian, rabbit, turtle. The man I ran into once,
a namesake, paced himself around an uphill bend,
the weak leg lagging behind. *Recovering*
from a stroke, he said, his speech slurring.

A policeman questions a young girl about her
binoculars. She's a birder. There are about
ten varieties of ducks on this wetland. The hawk
climbs into a sky suddenly dark and ominous.

Fanfare

Let's turn tonight upside down
and find what was lost so long ago,
let's keep the corners moving and
look down the empty side streets
that run into the traffic roaring.
Let's go into diners where two
or three sip their coffee slowly,
where a melancholy light plays
on blue muffins and our pins
sparkle as we come in and
run back out again.

Let's look up at the stars, stars
that are there when we remember,
and run through the alleys and burst
upon the thoroughfare holding our sides,
let's take a livery cab uptown, pacing
ourselves in store windows, yellow
lights and mannequins, until we don't
know where we are, like the river,
flowing north or south, and someone
calls out, *Hey, lady, hey mister!*

We're all grown up now; we can go
where we want, and stay as long.
Let's look in the water at our reflection,
and still as herons see ourselves
turn silver as the sky behind us.
Let's go under the trees where shadows
still embrace and all together

lift the edge of night and find
the hollow of kisses, let's run through
it, turning the benches over and over.

Stiff Upper

In a newspaper kiosk, the Indian seller
ducked when he heard the first bomb go off,

and in the smoke-filled exit from the underground,
a bobby bled from one ear and switched his radio

to the other. In Hyde Park, the speaker forgot what
he was going to say, as into the Immigration Office

pigeons flew, scattering application forms.
And then the bus, oh, the bus bound for Piccadilly

made an unprecedented leap across the intersection,
the conductor stern-faced in the open air, the roof

and the upper level blown off, all of England
bloody well blaming the Irish before realizing

this was a brand new conflict, and that
had been a different war.

A Well-Bred Woman

1.

She leaps to her feet
condemning the cops
who shot her son.

She turns into something
primitive, screaming
the American word

for a man
who sleeps
with his mother,

puts her hand
over her mouth as
she hears the gates open,

and they are let out
to walk on the grass
outside the courthouse

where no lion waits
to eat them, though
she prayed for one,

no owl hooted
in the noonday sun,
no calamity befell

the black sedan that
drove away with them
down the highway.

2.

The reporters ask
and she tells them,
in my country, Amadou

is a common name. It is
like stones in the road.
And there are many

fathers named Diallo,
who all run out when
they hear the drums

say, your son,
your son, your son
Amadou. They look

everywhere—in the home,
in the compound,
in the cassava field

down by the river
where the crocodiles
steal the goats—

they search until they
remember the one
who went to America,

then they hug
the remaining Amadous—
and weep.

Casualties

In human terms, the cost is high.
The earth will have to dig in her purse
like an old woman, or the butcher
will take back his meat.

Perhaps it won't be so bad. She can wrap
herself in leaves and eat the tomatoes
that burst their thin skins, She can squat
near palaces in cities built of her own clay.

She can follow the armies that take her dirt
to bury their dead. She can swallow her pride,
pockmarked and disguised as a refugee,
she can sit in a camp. Or, a pretty blue marble,

she can smile in the eye of one whose hobby
is astronomy, spinning with her sun and
moon, day and night sucking salt
through a wooden spoon.

Remember

If we meet again, after this,
on some street corner,
or in a marketplace
in some foreign country

when the bombs
have stopped dropping
and you balance a beautiful
baby in one hand while

testing melons with the other,
if we stand there in the hubbub
each staring and saying
how much the other has changed

or looks the same,
if I don't remember your name
as I introduce you to someone
who has befriended me and

stands patiently while we recall
days when the world had
gone crazy, and you asked me
who would save it,

remember I said, you will,
even if I leave, even if you never
hear from me again, you'll
find someone to tell your story,

who will get word to the front
that the war is over and the children
can go back to the classroom now,
who will find me

wherever I am, in the mountains
or by the sea, waiting
and listening for the quiet
that will let us think, and when

we walk from each other,
you by way of the oranges, me
by the fish, my friend will look back,
as I remember your name.

~NO BACK DOOR~

(2010)

The Center of the World

1.

From here I can see the world, all the people
walking down Flatbush Ave., going into stores,
waiting at the bus stop, all the latecomers rushing
into the subway cat-a-corner from my window,
across Ocean Ave., all the new immigrants in winter
wearing too much clothes, the police recruit from
Long Island under the awning of the Arab grocer.

Salaam, I can hear the crack addict, the last of
his kind disappearing between the floorboards,
arguing with the Arab chief, the one with the scar
on his left cheek, next door to whom the Asians
scrape calluses from feet three times the size
of their own, giving them the designs they want:
star, crescent, half-moon, the flag of any country.

I see all four seasons pass through the park, in
winter the lake shimmering between the trees,
in autumn the nervous leaves shaking and falling,
the sudden flood of green in spring. And summer,
O Summer, with the smoke of a hundred grills,
the smell of barbecue, the birthday balloon sailing
away from a crying boy, the slap of dominoes
on the picnic tables, the relentless hawk, a rat

dangling from its talons, blood dripping onto a
cyclist's jersey, the yellow paddleboats on their
circular journey around the island that is the ducks'
breeding ground, dense, impenetrable, the raccoon

that scared us after the concert at the bandshell
the night Rudder sang his calypso blues, where
a year ago Odetta made her last appearance, half-
sitting under a falling moon. And the vet whose
shock of white hair stood out among the runners,
I don't hear his sidewise shout anymore.

In the zoo the enclosure where the bears ate a boy
one summer has a higher fence, painted with pretty
pictures. On Sundays the drummers still form their
rings, and in the evenings, horns announce the arrival
of the Haitians, their sound atonal, harsh, unrelieved.
They move in concentric circles, singing not words
but a series of o's, rising, falling, rising.

2.

Sometimes the midnight lines at the McDonald's are
seven registers across. Here a homeless man might sit,
nursing coffee, pretending to wait for the No. 12.
I know where it goes, out Linden, through dangerous
parts of East New York. I take it almost to the end of
the line, to a building boasting a thirteenth floor and
terraces with a great view of flights leaving Kennedy.

I watch the Puerto Ricans on their day, the *coquís*
on the hatband of the older men. On Fridays the Jews
stream in numbers toward the end of the park where
the big synagogue is, the cops with backs to them
blocking traffic. I see all the time accidents happen
at this five-way intersection, an elderly couple never
making it to a wedding, their car spun round to face
the opposite way. I catch, on Labor Day,

steelpans going down the middle of the avenue,
a girl waving a mysterious flag, the sergeant longest
on the beat saying, *Ah, don't worry 'bout it, too long
to explain what wining is.* I've heard relationships die
at 3 a.m. among the pillars in the pavilion, or at the stoplight,
while a car idled. I've heard the prettiest rendition of
a Scott Walker song come up the fire escape and through
my window, "through a long and sleepless night … "

3.

I've heard the shocking quarrels of people over
a parking space, over love, over nothing. I've seen
a boy gasp his last between the park benches
after the pop, pop turned out not to be fireworks,
the cap on his head turning red. There are times
I look out to see not a soul, and times it seemed
a congregation had gathered under my window,
times when the heat would rise and then would not,
my guest and I sleeping in gloves.

I've lived through three supers, watched their sons
grow to manhood. I've let my next door neighbor
climb through my window when she'd forgotten
her keys. I've stepped over the nodding ghosts
of addicts acting like doormen in the lobby, their
number dwindling till there was one, who could
hardly lift my suitcase. I leave but always come back
here, where I review things from this vantage point,
the confluence of people and lives after deliveries
are dropped off early in the morning by trucks
rambling through this intersection of the world.

Stutterstep

Old men don't stagger because they're
drunk, their legs just don't go where
they want them to. They look distracted
because they're thinking about some
things they could have done differently.

Old men are fools for wondering how
they got here, when they started out
for somewhere else, even had a map.
They retrace their steps and stand at
the crossroads, looking this way and that.

They almost get run over, not by young
punks, but by other old men whose shirts
are buttoned the wrong way, who
slap away the wife's hand, insisting they
can do it themselves. They call a friend

and, when he no longer answers, they
cradle the phone quietly, emitting one
of those long sighs that only a lover
from the distant past can hear, she who
died in the back of a taxicab or suddenly

on a cruise somewhere out in the middle
of the Atlantic when their song was playing.
Old men do the stutterstep, a kind of dance
that comes naturally to them, a hesitation,
while the feet try to figure the next move.

Newsboy

for my son

I'm sorry I didn't go with you
on your rounds, that it was your mother who
had to drive in the predawn hour behind you,

that it was her you drove crazy as you
folded each paper, fussing with rubber bands
while she waited, pajamas under her housecoat.

She told me how you'd walk down
the sloping yards of West Covina and place
the daily carefully on each veranda,

then back out to your bike and get on,
instead of tossing the paper like the other boys,
how much you reminded her of your damn father.

The Stowaway

for Happy

She was that kind of mother.
When the captain brought you up
to the bridge, your skinny legs knocking
in the new trousers, questioning you

about the stowaway hidden in your room,
whose passport was found by the cleaning crew,
who had stood on deck with the rest of the
passengers waving, you thought the ship

would turn around and take you back
in shame, in distress, to face the neighbors.
But the captain announced the only reason
he wouldn't prosecute was that your mother

had spoken to him when you boarded,
that he should look after her son, who of late
was getting beside himself, and for her sake
and hers alone, he'd let you sail on to England.

When did she do that, you wondered,
how did she know the way to the captain's
room, let alone his heart, she who had never
left the port of Port of Spain, who

stayed in her room and made costumes for
plays at the Little Carib, and saved this coat
from the time your sister took her first trip,
so you would be warm when you landed.

Traveling Song

for Sekou Sundiata

That night in the park when Odetta sang
"Alabama Bound," I thought I saw your hat
move through the crowd, thought I
heard you call for a microphone. Then

everything got so still. Odetta sang
that traveling song, the glare
from her dress made me close my eyes,
and the white kid made that stride piano

sound like a train moving through the dark.
Odetta did like she was waving from
a window, and you were coming down the aisle.
Last stop, you whispered, without slowing down.

He Loved Calypso

They say you shouldn't look
at the casket as it goes into
the fire at the crematorium.

Some people faint, some
feel the heat long afterwards,
unable to dispose of the ashes.

After they wheeled Freddie in,
I could see through the ovals
of the closed double doors

the great hook of his nose,
the silver clasp holding his tie,
and the two pictures someone

had placed on his chest—one
of Sparrow, the other of Rose—
before both burst into flame.

Man in the Back

There's a man who lives
in the house in the back.
He is there by himself
with his thoughts and

words he writes to
express them. A little dog
has befriended him. It
sleeps behind the sofa,

waiting for him to
come out of his trance.
They go round the Savannah,
people complimenting

the dog, telling the man
to shorten the chain when
it becomes difficult
to control the animal.

Back in the house the man
is grateful for the chance
to have been seen
doing an ordinary task.

For all his work with words,
a simple thing like
naming the dog eludes him.
Dog, he calls him, *dog*.

Jealousy

for Fitzroy Coleman

Once, he entertained royalty in London.
His playing is said to have made
Marlene Dietrich swoon.

Now he tends a garden in Toco,
bending among his plants and listening
to the earth play back its melodies.

Those who want to learn he teaches
on an old guitar whose fret the damp
has put almost past mending.

Late at night, neighbors say, he plays
a strange ballad, about a country girl who
came to the city, asking back for her keys.

The Importance of a Man Like Sammy

He's been living in his mother's house
somewhere in the hills above Caracas
ever since those days in Brooklyn,
when his second wife drove him crazy.

Or it could have been the partying, a girl
getting shot in the backseat of his car.
But now he's back, recalling everything,
having little trouble keeping names

and circumstances straight. He
paces up and down in a shared room
while *sotto voce*, someone mentions that
he has had an operation, that now

there's a tube in his head. But Sammy's
still Sammy, captain of the old Silk Hats
gang, still has that hyper way of reminding
us, we were either villains or heroes, never

ordinary. And while he rambles on, eyes
faraway and Spanish with intensity, we
stare at the scar on the side of his head
where they must have slipped it in.

Felicity

after Derek Walcott

The Indian father killed the black boy
he thought had threatened his son.
And the black men said that for this,
twenty Indians would have to die.

And they pulled drivers from their vehicles,
and people boarded themselves up inside
their houses, and fires blazed at every
intersection of Felicity, the village

immortalized by the poet in his speech,
when he won the Nobel, as a place
of magic and great beauty, the dancers
having left an indelible impression

on his mind. He spoke as if he
were still standing at the edge of the field
where they had performed, where,
in the stalled traffic yesterday,

some men broke a windshield and pulled
a woman from her car and cut off her hair.
And the army patrolled the country roads
day and night, the scent of jasmine overtaken

by the smell of fear. It's a different Felicity
now, one that never occurred to the poet as
he described the hands that skimmed oil
from the heads of the dancers and

rubbed their legs till they glistened. He'd
thought only of how such rapture might
spread to the neighboring villages, and
from them outward and upward,

a gift to the rest of the world.

Dawn, at the Home

I ask for you, and the nurse
leads me into the lounge.

You're the youngest person there.
I sit next to you, and take your hands.

The minute I let go, you pretend
to be washing again.

The attendant reminds me that
you can't see, and that even if

you could, you wouldn't know me.
I come closer to you.

We made love once,
I whisper as a last resort.

Payday at Chaguaramas

On the American base, everything
looked dangerous: the bay scooped out
for submarines, the .45 on the hip of soldiers,
the engines they took apart in dark hangars.

Once, the marine who stood guard
as we paid the locals didn't show up, and
the new guy told us he was in the jailhouse
for wounding another man. That day on the long lines,

whenever someone grew restless or mumbled
that a pay packet was short, our new escort's hand
went for his gun, and we missed Joe, who was much
more patient, speaking with that slow, easy drawl.

Refugees

At some dawn in a shallow cove
they arrive, the water whitening
as they come ashore and
bed down on the sand.

In sleep their bodies
do a rowing motion,
the muscles of the men
tugging the oars in the darkness.

No one knows where they are.
Right now they have
the fishes' memory, and
as soldiers appear

on a horizon of dry coconuts,
the group on the sand
waits to hear the name
of what country they're in.

~THE WAVING GALLERY~

(2014)

The Waving Gallery

Up there, I could make out my mother
in her favorite dress, the one she wore
in pictures taken thirty years apart, and

Doris, her best friend who'd warned her
not to cry. Behind them stood Uncle Freddie,
waving the keys to the house and the Hillman.

Across the tarmac, the line of passengers
moved slowly. Looking up, the hills seemed
closer. I thought I could make out people

in houses, children in yards who could
see me going away to study English, as
if it were not the language spoken here.

Mt. Hololo

for LeRoy Clarke

Let's talk, my friend,
when the wind comes
across the mountain
to touch our faces, and

flowers in your yard
rise on their stems
to salute, and the cock
puffs the feathers

round his neck, the
hens walking away
as if to say not again,
not today. Let's

talk about winters
in far-off lands, irate
husbands and windows
we jumped from,

let's break the deck
and play a game of
Go-to-Pack, though
neither of us is any

good. Show me
a painting you've
been working on,
that may or may not

be going well. Let's
argue about a line,
a verse in a poem, the
cause of a fire that

has suddenly bloomed
on the hill. Let's leave
some issues for another
day, otherwise what

would we do tomorrow,
when your rooster's
tail grows too heavy for
his body, and the ladies

must remind him
when it's time to crow.
Let's discuss, until then,
important matters,

like the estimated
age of your eldest
turtle, like the day
that is dying outside.

First Time Seeing Snow

There's that scene in the movie when Sinatra
shuts off the wipers and floors the accelerator.

You feel like a passenger. You can't see a thing.
You hear the tick of ice hitting the windshield,

the whine of the motor, and you think of the song
he sang back in the bar—"One for My Baby."

You yell, *Don't do it, man. Doris loves you, the way*
you looked when she answered the door, that hat …

The car's an old Ford and in the theater, your foot
mashes the brake long after you've struck a tree.

And you sit there, Frankie slumped over the steering,
snow thick and heavy under the tires, churning.

Marie, and Juan

If he'd stayed in his country
and you in yours, you'd never
have danced like this.

He would never have crossed
the border between the cane,
nor known your name.

Your memory of Trujillo
would have kept your eyes
focused on a machete,

and your cry in patois
would've brought your father
running, the old Boukman record

skipping on the gramophone.
But here you are, dancing a
bachata in Brooklyn.

The step is fast,
that zombie from the past
trying to catch up.

And Now This

for Edwidge Danticat

Sometimes it must feel like
your fight for independence
will never end, that liberty
will keep eluding you like
a goat that runs into the sea.

The preacher says it is your
voudou that is killing you,
that keeps you scraping and
digging and having to subdue
the enemy in your own house.

But who can deny you your
home, where even in hunger
your mouths sing and drums
beat the sweetest ra-ra,
where your soldiers once

marched over the cliffs to
their death in the sea. And now
this, your roof falling in while
you were combing a daughter's
hair, sending her off to school,

while you opened your stall
to sell the few grains that still
manage to grow, here comes
a rain of rocks upon your head,
a shaking of the ground, as if

God doesn't know his own
strength, as if he were dancing
in his house above the mountain
where the cries of so many
voices could not reach.

But who could pretend
not to hear such
a breaking up of earth,
such a tear and
a split run all the way

from Petionville to Jacmel,
through the heart of
Port-au-Prince, that where
it ended, it seemed it
could never be joined again.

A whole new island I tell you
is what you need—new roof,
new flooring, new everything,
new hills, new flowers, new
yard with no fence to say

this is yours, that is theirs,
someone forever claiming
what you worked so hard for.
A place you can bring all those
boat people back to, where

you can make a big bonfire of
all the bad memories, of Papa
This and Baby That, the furry

slippers of all their madams.
But never mind my wishes.

This is where you are now.
This is your sweet and sour, your
grief on top of grief, your little
girl dancing to show the amputation
was a success. Amazing how

you sing through your sorrow,
how you still fling your behind
in the Carnival, and say your
prayers, however you remember
them, whatever sacrifice

you must make: chicken,
goat, your own blood, saying,
Not me, not my Ayiti, blood
coming out of her pores.
Her mountains march up

and down beside the river
that divides the island as you
put it back together, the plates
that shifted the day the world
broke into a million pieces.

The Old Ways

in memory of Chinua Achebe

I would travel north to hear the great writer
whose story about the champion wrestler
Okonkwo set the bar so high, no rival
could take him down. If I still had

a girlfriend living there, I would spend
the weekend in Providence, finding it
hard to get decent fish in a city so near
the sea. I could bear anything, the steep,

narrow staircase up to her bedroom, the
mattress on the attic floor. But now I hear
Chinua has died, I don't think I could stand
the sound of her roommates' chatter.

It brings to mind the children of the Evil
Forest, thrown there for being different. So I
stay home and reread how nightly, the hero chose
which wife, by placing his stool outside her door.

Single File

for Brenda Connor-Bey

Last night the stars came out
as never before, in clusters,
one in particular flashing
its brilliance, its size. And we

interpreted this as a sign, as
powerless people tend to do, of
heaven's willingness to let us
have a few more minutes to say

what we have to say, to locate
an address we once knew
by heart. And this is how we
come to *her* door, single file,

no one anxious to precede
another, as in all her grace
she slips out a window, shinnies
down a drainpipe, gone. Who,

for all our calling, won't come back,
will have us look up, on nights
like this, gazing at stars, believing
we know exactly which one she is.

Language Major

Underneath the Calvert Street Bridge, our
roommate Peter and a white woman who
looked younger in the bar, both tipsy, are
going at it. It's snowing hard, the bridge

a postcard scene lit by antique streetlamps,
the windows of the Hotel Shoreham alive
with chatter and the tinkle of silverware.
The sounds of Peter's grunts echo loudly

from the underpass, the woman, her coat
and dress bunched at the waist, suddenly
declaring she doesn't like Negroes.
You're Spanish, aren't you? she mutters.

And Dr. P (as we called him), ever mindful,
even in distress, whispers, *Sí, sí,* snow
blowing down the steep embankment
into his ear, and onto his exposed behind.

Concern

The forceps left two bruises
on my son's head, visible till
he was about six weeks old.

What kind of doctor, I ask,
grabs a kid like that, pulls him
like meat from the grill when

it's done? Two green spots,
as if the tongs were old, the
first thing they could find.

I find myself looking, now
the boy's over forty, for further
signs of damage. So far, none.

The Last Round

for Neal

This is what happened after doctors said
there was nothing more they could do, after
he'd flown back and forth across the Atlantic.

He went home and sold everything—furniture,
clothes, car. Opened the gate and let the two
Dobermans out: *Go, run for your lives!*

Lately, when he speaks, his voice is a rasp,
that powerful neck closed around it like a bell
around the clapper, and his speech is slurred.

There's no fooling a fighter, especially the one
he faces now, who keeps his hood on till the last
minute, who closes in, knowing the dogs are gone.

Manuel

The Spanish guy who lives downstairs
recently lost his wife. I miss seeing them
out front, her wheelchair angled against
the stoop, his eyes tired from staying up.

In my bad Spanish I'd quip, *Cómo estás?*
her *mucho dolor* turning the evening purple,
like her hands on her knees. Since her death
he sits alone, announcing he has a dryer

and a washing machine for sale. And a
freezer, he adds, showing the dimensions
by extending his arms, a gesture that seems
both an offer to hug, *and* the size of his pain.

Sedona

By now the desert air
should have calmed your fears.
Mine are still rock-hard—if
nothing else, good for building fences.
In Arizona, if I recall rightly,
standing close to the saguaro brings
a sense of euphoria. Have you done that yet?

When you lived at the Y on Lexington
in that cupboard of a room, you'd
cut the neck off a Pepsi bottle so I could pee.
I imagine where you are now I could stand
at your back door and spray the stars and send
the peccaries scooting back into the hills.

I picture your dad, old army man
in his trailer with his collection of bottle caps,
what he would do if he ever saw your white
legs wrapped around me, how he would
fasten the door so I couldn't leave, he and
your mother closing her gas station in Baltimore
to spend Thanksgiving with your brother in Virginia,
discussing your topless cleaning job, chastising
their daughter-in-law for being overweight
next to their gelding son.

I'd come visit you where you are now,
far from the family, undoing whatever
side effects years of medication have produced.
But having never gone to Pittsburgh where

you drank so much water you gurgled when you walked,
I doubt I'll make it to Sedona, out there among
the spas and retreats, practicing the mountain mantras,
deep breath and hold, deep breath, hold.
I'd probably find myself asking about
those scratches on your lower back, as if you'd
lain on the desert floor somewhere, in your dress
full of stars streaking across a midnight sky.

Countryside

As many times as I've been there,
the roads remain strange, going east
when I think we're headed south,
passing fields of farmers
who shake their head.

I was born here, though
when I put out my hand, the fish
swim away. The men toast someone
with rum behind a partition, and
only one aunt welcomes me.

In the yards behind houses
rain falls in buckets, and
a quiet holds the hills like rakes
at lunchtime. I forget which trace
leads to the sea, innocent

waves washing away the sand:
Manzanilla, Mayaro, Gasparee. Only
fifty square miles, but it can go on
forever, machetes looking for
something to cut, besides cane.

The Devil's Chariot

Old Mr. Headley, Gospel Hall pastor, when
my aunt asked what kind of car she should get,
said the automobile was the devil's chariot.

But those deuce-and-a-quarter winged ones
lining the church driveway belonged to him
and his sons, the men as they passed remarking

that the steering columns were on the left.
When church was over, and Mr. Headley sat
with the motor running, his radio tuned to

a religious station from nearby Venezuela,
he wondered what made Charlotte think
she could afford one, as she brushed past,

bangles jangling, bending to check her
face in one of his side mirrors, making sure
her hat with the long feather was on straight.

John Creig, Esquire

He came in his rags
to the post office, letter
addressed to the Queen.

He had just enough for
postage, everyone admiring
his handwriting, how wonderful.

How long, he inquired,
would it take to get there?
Four weeks, said the clerk,

placing the letter where
all crazy correspondence went,
in a bin, filled to the top.

Stella

In old age she has become
as fluent in Spanish as she was
when she was twenty, still living
in that village south of Caracas.

All grown up, her children are
amazed at how she keeps their
uniforms, as if someday they
might have to go back to school.

And her husband who first
taught her English observes
how she has shrunk to just
below his tunic pocket, she

who used to see eye to eye
with him on everything, like
never using profanity in front
of the kids, now saying,
Besa mi culo, to everyone.

Widow's Peak

It comes to the edge
of the forehead,

that diving wedge,
the mark of a man

who will outlive his wife.
My father had one,

a plunging arrowhead
aligned with his nose.

Stubborn to the end,
he went first,

a cynic who had
no faith in signs.

Facing Montrose

When I was five, we moved to a house
diagonally across the street, with
an iron bathtub in the yard. We

carried things by hand, the light stuff
my mother and I, the big press
my uncle and a man in a heavy jacket.

It was temporary, until my dad
finished building the one in the lane
facing Montrose. *Careful with the teapot,*

my mother said, excitement in her eyes.
Would we bathe outside for all the neighbors
to see, would my father finally, after

parking his bike in the new yard, hang
his uniform behind the door and stay, instead
of riding away, down the hill in the dark?

~VOICES CARRY~

(2017)

Pops, Fathers, Uncle

These are my new names, given me by complete strangers. Suddenly I'm related to the young man who moves over in the taxi, to the girl clerking in the clothing store who asks,

Uncle, you getting through?

I suppose I am. I've come through crowded Port of Spain, misjudged a high pavement, at the last minute catching myself. I've managed to remember where the taxi stand is on Charlotte St., waiting till I hear, *Belmont, Fathers?* I look around for a cleric collar, for the priest who must have been put out from the Cathedral, which is being renovated. How do all these people think me family, from the Rasta selling fruit, quietly rolling his blunt, to the Indian shaving fins from the cro cro I just bought. In what ways do we resemble?

I take the seatbelt the woman in the backseat is shaking to remind me, *Buckle up, Daddy.* I snap it in and catch a glimpse of her in the rearview mirror. She's at least as old as I am. I'm tempted to say, *Thank you, daughter.* But instead I say, *Thank you, dear. Thank you.*

A Kind of Valentine

in memory of Asami Nagakiya

I think of somewhere safe
to take you if you should come to visit,
if I should tell you about the body

found among the poui blossoms
of the murdered girl who'd come
from Japan to play the steelpan.

I will walk you round this Savannah,
because we always boast of its beauty,
and because it's where all our love

and all our craziness take place,
where horses have raced and rapists
greased to the belly have crept

and come upon careless couples.
You should be safe during the day,
when thousands are around. But

I'll show you where not to go at night.
Remember it's Carnival, and behind the masks,
men are not always who they say they are.

Not Cricket

My poet friend has grown careless.
He's in love, and metaphors abound.
Now when he writes of revolution
and struggle, the lines waver, turn

to descriptions of her curves, kisses
thrown in her direction falling back
to earth, like bombs falling on
a field outside Jaffna, where first

he learned the game of cricket,
the danger of a ball that almost
took out an eye. When she grows
angry enough to break his glasses,

he pretends they're playing, runs up,
imagines he's throwing rockets to
help the rebels defend the besieged
borders in the northern provinces.

Sometimes, listening to her breathe
after they make love, he wonders
if they'll ever move the barriers,
if his words would ever reach

the encampments where the Tigers
are hemmed in, while his eyes
sweep the darkened room, his
poems scattered under her bed.

Vangi Goes Home

She's going back to hear stories
about boys sent up the mountains

for initiation, some of whom
never return. She's going to look

for a friend last seen pushing a cart
like a vagrant. We will miss her, but

she must go back to the country
where they make that click sound,

where women walk like scorpions,
stingers in the air. She's going

to help prepare those potions
that show others the way home.

Crazy Ursula

for Brens, in memory

I remember your excitement showing me
the kurta you found at the bazaar:
Fifteen dollars, imagine, fifteen!

And I joked, where would you put it,
with the rest of the things that left
no room for us in the bed? It was so

sheer, standing before the light you looked
like Crazy Ursula naked by the standpipe,
after the man stole her money and ran Venezuela.

Lemongrass

Nature can't decide this evening, snow or rain.
We watch it come down, and order everything
on the menu, my grandson identifying the vehicle
splashing by outside as not just truck, but flatbed.

He chews the duck, flies his plate off the tarmac of
the table. Gates 45 and 92, Grandma badgering him
with questions. I sit at the far end, happy for the family.
How could I ever have rejected this, for some imagined
adventure, cardboard creatures folding in the rain?

We taste each other's food—the curry, the ginger,
the coconut, the green ice cream. My daughter-in-law's
belly almost touches the table, a second child.
I'm here, I'm gone away, swimming back
for everything I left behind, adding a line

to the toast they ask me to make. *Salud,*
dear family, forgive me for coming in and out
of your vines, but look how beautiful you are, twined and
running along each other's bones, new growth urging you on.

The Birthday Boy

My brother's in his nineties now,
and I'm thinking, should I continue
our hundred-dollar exchange this
year, me sending him one in late
August, he in December sending it
back, broken into twenties? Why

bother, I'm saying, I could just
get a bottle of rum and head out
to Queens, although lately he has
to hide to take a drink, since his
bout with gout, his wife keeping
an eye on him, her pacemaker

forcing him to go easy. How about
a hat, I consider, though he hardly
goes anywhere now, and doesn't
fuss much about how he looks.
In the picture on my dresser, people
who come over think he's a movie

star, black Paul Newman, I kid you
not. It was taken back when he was
an up-and-coming welterweight.
His girlfriend Lucille was a beauty
with a whispery voice you had to
come close to hear and doing so,

you'd catch a whiff of that perfume.
Come to think of it, what could I

get him that's better than what he's
already had. I confess I followed them
one night, just to see where you'd
take a lady like that, lucky guy.

Death in Mudland

Poor Professor Perry, what did they
think to find, those thieves running
from your residence, besides books
left over from teaching days in wintry
states, a bottle of preserved plums,

the icebox door ajar. What, climbing
those rickety stairs, did they imagine
the portrait of your wife on the landing
might fetch from a deal in Georgetown,
US or GT dollars exchanged in the old

wooden quarters of that city. What of
worth, their beady eyes dancing, did
they believe they'd discover in your
suitcase on the unmade bed in a back
room, half unpacked, dumb witness

to their crime—shirts spread about,
striped ties, graded papers and
an army of letters intended for
friends that they'll never receive.
Only news of your sad death, of

the heat and humidity, of the robbers
in hurried scamper from your house.
Like rodents, one reporter said,
among them three who seemed to be
females, judging by their long tails.

~COUNTRY OF WARM SNOW~

(2020)

Status

Sheriff, the African tailor on Flatbush,
wants to learn English. He can speak
it but not write it. He's from Conakry,

a word so wonderful I say it again—
Conakry. I offer him slips on which
to write the names of customers

so he does not mix up the clothes.
When we converse, I find myself
imitating his accent, asking him

where he learned tailoring skills so
remarkable. The space where he sews
is like a cupboard, his four countrymen

squeezed in behind him. We discuss
our cultures, and talk about these
new immigration laws, how they

affect so many. I have no idea what
his status is. I only know that when
I stand before the mirror, my old suit

looks new, and that I would hide him
in my house and feed him whatever
kind of soup it is they love over there.

Begging a Lodging

1.

Between two buildings hangs a half-moon,
sparks rising from the fire over which we
tune our pans. But no matter how sweet

the sound, the neighbors call the police.
When they come, we let the fair-skinned guy
speak for us, his accent taking the Americans

by surprise. One homeowner calls us foreign,
says we piss on her flowers. The half-moon
floats like an island, in and out of focus.

2.

Down in the basements, where immigrants
hide, the sky seems smaller, cut into rooms that
share a kitchen, a bath at the end of the hall.

And when someone asks whatever happened
to so-and-so, we shake our head, only to hear
a week later, he was found half-off the bed,

dead, the smell like oysters gone bad, and on
the nightstand a manila envelope, in it an old
passport and an enlarged x-ray of his heart.

3.

One morning I met my cousin on the cheese
line, outside a neighborhood church. When
I scolded that it was meant for the poor, he

said, *This country has plenty to go around.*
This is why we came, for the chance to beg
a lodging, for the moon, for the green cheese.

Aretha

In Port of Spain the taxi driver said
the woman on the radio singing
"Respect," was Carla Thomas.

That's Aretha, I said.

He said, I meant to say, Aretha,
their voices sound so similar.
She used to sing with Otis.
No, I said, Otis sang with Carla.

Her daddy was Rufus.
He sang "Walking the Dog."
In DC, I saw her play his record
on a jukebox, quarter after quarter.

That Aretha, said the cabbie,
she's something else.

Seven Beauties, Remembered

In South Trinidad one day,
a man walked past
the refinery guard,

climbed a ladder and
dove into a tank of crude.
It took days to recover

his heartbroken body,
days of stirring until he
bobbed to the surface.

It took him longer
than it did the prisoner
in a Nazi compound

who ran between
the lines of inmates
and officers, diving

into a dumpster
full of human waste,
a move that left you

with your mouth open
long after the film
had moved on

to the next scene,
with Giannini trying
in vain to fuck the fat

female commandant,
her heel digging
into his bare shoulder,

hardly able
to perform,
so weak he was.

Parables

When my friend LeRoy decided to leave America,
I remember him getting a haircut that last day,
sitting in a chair in the middle of his living room,
the rest of the furniture shipped or sold, only his
plants still hanging in windows and from shelves.

I watched the barber take his time as the sextons
in the churchyard across the street folded their tents,
their parables enticing no more visitors; they carried
poles and canvas carefully, like patients, closing
the heavy church doors behind them. This, I

thought, is the season that marks the end of things.
I remember looking at the bare walls, and LeRoy,
when asked about the plants, saying, *Let them die.*
His paintings, unframed and rolled, were out in
the hallway packed in boxes, like long boats.

March of the Children

There are many gods: god of sunlight,
god of the brook, god of night, god of rain,
god of the child who comes to see what
I'm doing, god of the mother who cries,

Leave him alone! God in the sulfur of the
match, god in the ashes, god of silence
who lets only the crickets chirp, god who
places antlers on the deer, god of ivory,

and of wood. Good gods, they all crowd
outside our window when we pray, gods
of debate and argument and rhyme, fire
gods, less inclined to talk lest they cause

conflagration. They come in answer to
our children's present prayer, since it's
not the usual call for sneakers, or a toy,
or for a boy to like me, or for longer hair,

but for an end to war, for god of mongoose
to stop it from killing a snake, for Anansi
to stop telling stories, the schoolyard today
empty, as if everyone has a fever, the god

of islands pushing them all together like
desks, so the children can copy from
each other the lesson *On Disobedience,*
on when the children are no longer ours,

so they're free to leave home in a dinghy
and paddle till all the boats are met in the
Ocean of Plastics and from there proceed
to the giant Oil Spill and the ice melting

like ice cream while we keep saying no,
it was the other god we meant, the one
who fixes what we break, the one who has
no designation but to see about us fools,

god of enigma god of folly god of cars that
drive themselves god of ducks and deer
crossing the highway have mercy on them
on the children as they feed us in our dotage

wipe our mouths our behinds our slates
clear of wrongdoings, shame and misdeeds,
our money-god the last to come, the one who
called for children to be caged, that ungod.

Fatherhood

for Ihsan

It helps if your father's a poet and
read you sonnets, if one happened
to stay in your head, guiding you
through this maze that is life.

If he dedicated one of his books
to you, even if you were too young
to take in a single line, you could
come later to understand the whole
thing was one long apology for what
seemed like selfishness on his part,

the way you yourself are accused
of being distant, always rehearsing
under your breath how a word fits,
compared to another. And though

there are no excuses for letting
my son wait by himself in a motel
for his mother to come from work
as she made a new start in California,
no poem worthy of the images

of dunes in the distance, of that
empty pool round back, they form
as if I had looked out with you,
the way a poem will lay down lines
for a train to run, and a platform
where we wait, in case one is coming.

Treasury Days

for Benji

Perhaps it's for the best you're not
around today to hear the mistakes
I might make, my memory never
as good as yours when we had to

go over columns of figures in
that granite building at the bottom
of St. Vincent Street, new clerks in an
old government. That was when

balancing the books was our biggest
problem. That, and liking a woman
whose husband had horses. What was
her name again? After all these years,

there's no detail you can't recall.
Like the last time we sat—you, me,
and the nurse, around the table
where your meds were lined up

so there'd be no error, so you could
retrieve the one for sugar, the one for
pain—and blind, could still picture the
shirt someone on a given day was wearing.

The School Gate

1.

Before reaching her, her killer
passed many people: a fishmonger,
whose blade was longer than his,

the Muslim entering the mosque,
its turrets gleaming in the sunlight,
a grandmother, hurrying the kids off to school,

and the owners of an antique shop, where
the schoolmistress had found a rocker
to match her chairs.

2.

At the school gate, she had the children
line up: boy-girl-boy, greeting them, unaware
of his presence. And as they stood

staring, mouths open, superhero
lunchboxes dangling from their arms,
they witnessed his stabbing motion,

while she never screamed, only kept
pointing at the entrance they should go in—
Please, dear God, go in. Go in.

After the Flood

Only babies slept through the howling winds.
Morning finds the madman absent from his
post, though his bicycle bell keeps ringing.

The South is worse than the North; in some
quarters, no lights. It's also bad in Central,
where for now, the shooting has stopped.

Tomorrow, the clinics will reopen. Patients
will wait nervously for their chemo, observing
the lines to where the water came up. And

a badjohn, looking to settle a score, will hear
that the man's child has died, and will end up
helping him kill the snake found under the bed.

Men Only

The waiting room
at the prostate doctor's
is full of depressed-looking men
drinking extra cups of water

so they can pee
as the nurse stands behind them
with the instrument that measures
the girth of the penis

when you're done. The mind wills
the body to cooperate, the stream
to be strong. Later, before the intrusive
camera, your gland withdraws

as the technician tries
to distract you with stories
of her boyfriend who doesn't
like her doing this. *Breathe, she says.*

Outside, I recognize
more than one guy
from my neighborhood. We nod
disconsolately when the doc,

a sharp dresser, casually tells the nurse
to schedule someone for surgery.
The rest of us, relieved, toast each other
with more cups of water.

Resistance

The workmen are in my kitchen
tearing things apart. New cabinets,
though I loved the old country-style
ones, the scalloped trim I painted two

shades of blue. I hide out in the bedroom,
the walls shaking as they pound and
break wood that comes away with creaks
and groans, nails human in their holding.

Outside, it's a hot one, protesters
on the move. I feel compelled to mention
them, their bravery. Only yesterday
I came across a picture in the paper

of myself and students I'd encouraged
to march down a street in The Village.
It might have been for Mumia; the headline's
gone, and I don't remember the cause

exactly, or what we were yelling.
But now I'm thinking how
nothing gives way without breakage,
without some form of damage to the old,

the claw hammer in the hand of
the workman, the nail powerless as
he approaches. The battle for dignity rages
in the nights and days, the homeless joining

the campaign, the retired like me hunkered
down, taking notes, witnessing how there must
be dissent, and noise, the very floor coming up,
the policeman's foot in mid-kick, coming down.

Country of Warm Snow

for Courtenay

You stopped by, feet swollen
from sleeping sitting up.
I think of how we first made

our way across this country,
the state you got lost in—
was it east, west? Perhaps one

of the dry ones, like Nevada.
Never afraid to dream, your
idea of America remained what

we'd seen in movies: fields
where men keep rounding
the bases, cheeks red with

October chill. That first winter,
you said the snow looked warm.
And now someone's promised you

a cot in a basement, you grin with
delight, as if the offer has redeemed
whatever wrong was done to you.

Beloved

for Toni Morrison

The day you died, two deputies
led a black man into town
between their horses, spectators

lining both sides of the street,
recalling the days patterrollers
brought runaways back in chains,

the clanking heard long before
the captives appeared, like
this man, limping, the rope

round his wrists tied to the
pommel of one of the saddles.
His eyes, fixed on a place far away,

made us feel he could have been
in one of those novels of yours,
the child a mother had let live.

How They Looked

for Ansil & Peggy

All the years you were away
I kept that photo you sent,
standing by a big black car
with your wife Margaret,

you in a long winter coat,
she in a short fur. It was a
small, gray snapshot with
a white border, snow all over,

on the windscreen, on your
shiny black shoes, on the
windowsills of the building
behind you. I thought the car

was yours. Years later, when
you came home, you said
it wasn't. It just happened to be
on this wide street in Brooklyn

where the picture was taken,
when the snow seemed like
it would never melt, and
a good-looking guy and

a pretty lady stopped and
posed, leaning on the car,
and all the world for a second
looked like it belonged to them.

The Fight

for Keith & Ansil

The ad at Barclays Center is for
a fight between Deontay Wilder
and Luis Ortiz, and I thought you
guys would've liked to catch this,

arguing who had the uppercut,
who had the better jab, that
against Ali, neither would have
stood a chance. These are the

delights of the fight game:
the lacing up of the gloves,
the referee, the ringside crowd.
The sign has me thinking now

about how Ansil must have gone
headfirst down those stairs, his
grandson awakened in the basement
yelling, *Get up, Grandpa, get up!*

The way we call for the champ
to get up, while the corner man
who knows better, says, *Stay down,
son,* a bet none of us would've won.

My Father's Jacket

Hangs on a line outside, on a day
when it's snowing. The shoulders
are soon covered with white, his
body absent between the lapels.

It's how I dream him, in this
place where he has never been.
I speak to his shadow, his scent
strongest at the times I am idle.

In his quiet way, he takes note
of my silence, asks why I don't
go home to the house that rises
steeply at the back, as the steps

climb to meet the floor. It's where
I once fell into a bucket, my whole
body fitting, like a small animal. He
said, *Boy!* leaving me to my mother.

The jacket swings when the wind
blows, loose, dancing by itself, and
makes me remember the morning
of his funeral, when his friends sat

in the living room, and Telemaque,
his closest, asked if he could have
it, with its frayed cuffs and collar,
the two top brass buttons missing.

~NEWS OF THE LIVING~

(2020)

Day of the Virus

Behind a wall, small voices. Children
play unseen in an overgrown garden,
paving stones leading to a closed gate.

The wall around the garden is high.
They're safe from the madman who
walks into the grocery shouting for

things on his list: milk, Vienna sausage
his mother fixed him before she passed.
The children's game is magical—

mother-in-law tongues for swords, lilies
for hearts. They swash-and-buckle, and
have tea under an almond's broad leaves.

Sheltered from the virus now plaguing
the world, they sip and chat, using
adult words, like devastation.

Lockdown

In South Africa, under apartheid,
the old lady said, every day we were
stopped and asked to show our pass.

Isolation's not new to us, we've been
locked down a long time. Now we stay
inside, and sing songs about Madiba.

Because of him, the hospital has
to treat us—our sons and daughters
work there. They help turn the sick

face down, so all the patient sees are
the plastic covers on the doctors' shoes,
the bin in the far corner, overflowing.

News of the Living

Where's Leta, that I may hug and
greet her, her arms, her face white
with flour. She's been baking all day,

helping her son with the business.
Is the shop flourishing, the autistic
grandchild doing well? I can't think

whom else to inquire after, besides
Dudley, who long ago retired
into himself, drew the covers up

to his chin, as if he knew this day
was coming. Ah, Leta, I know you
are holding them all above water

while the floodgates of this virus
open around us. You'll convert
your house into boat, kitchen into

galley, beds into rafts, blowing into
the sails till your air runs out, then
fanning with your apron, fanning.

Small Wars

for Keith

After this battle with Covid-19,
we continue to fight smaller wars:

walk with the cancer patient
to chemo appointments, go

to the dialysis room where we
witness the bi-weekly transfer

of blood. Ask with hearts broken
as we encounter black men

shooting each other, *Do you*
not see ghosts swinging from trees?

And when our friend goes out
on these city streets in his

bathrobe, we are the ones
to bring him home

amid the protests and profiling,
who must remain among

the imaginary guests at
the foot of his bed

till they leave, and he feels
free to breathe again.

How to Grieve

Death has taken on
so many meanings. So many
bodies, we stop counting,

so many infected, we must
say goodbye from a distance.
And when a woman mounts

and straddles the coffin
of a dear one in an attempt
to love him back to life,

even while condemning
such a display,
we must forgive,

as we sing
Abide with Me,
silently urging her on.

She Sings in the Shower

Now in the fiftieth year of her sentence,
Gloria W., who tried when she was sixteen
to rob a store with her son's toy gun,

has appealed to the governor again. But
he has no time, the pandemic is spreading
all over Louisiana. So, she sings in the shower,

a song about a colored girl escaping through
the bayous, her child slung across her back,
and imagines her cellmates are grandchildren

gathered round, listening to her story
about snakes, and gators, and the virus
she caught in the swamp one time.

This Viral Season

Now the Botanic Gardens are closed,
the cherry blossoms bloom, but no one's
there to remark how early they arrived,

the pink carpet they leave on the grass.
The tropical trees, flamboyants and palms
lean in a greenhouse no one will visit

anytime soon. And in the gift shop, a
solitary clerk carefully wipes the shelves
and wares, the picture of a hybrid rose.

~THE LAST TRAIN~

(2023)

Gum

In American war movies, chewing gum was
a sign of staying calm while bullets whizzed
overhead, a sign of the kindness of GIs, as
they passed out sticks of it to wide-eyed kids.

In Minnesota, while a policeman kneeled on
George Floyd's neck, one of the officers kept
chewing as Floyd called to his deceased mom
that he was dying. And in Chicago, a black woman

just out the shower, stood in the middle of her
living room, shivering, the broken front door
letting in light, cops in a ring around her as she
screamed, *Wrong house, you got the wrong house!*

And though the sergeant used his jacket to try
and cover her, she'll never forget their faces,
especially the one who never stopped smiling
and chewing, who never once looked away.

War Days

Days of rations and shortages,
and the yellow ration card,
of lines outside Aleong's shop,
on the door the phrase—
Kilroy was here.

There were rumors of subs
in the sea all around, of enemies
embedded with us on this island
far from any bombing. It was not
our war. Still, Aunt Bertha sang,

Buy a Flanders poppy, save it
for a souvenir. When they ask
who you buying it for, say
Trinidadian boys who died
in the war. And we remained

as quiet as a blackout in Britain,
no Carnival for years, only
the Rediffusion crackling
with news and sailors in town
searching for the harbor,

while my father, responsible
for keeping the trains running,
on the way to work kissed
my mother as I insisted—
On the lips, Dad, on the lips.

The Poem as Train

I'm uncoupling the verses safely,
my father's severed thumb in mind.

The Rockies have stopped flashing by,
the Rio Grande has swallowed the moon.

I go from carriage to carriage, calming
passengers, one of whom says

he has to be in Philly by morning.
Only in the last stanza will I shout,

Boarrdd! As I've heard
the old man do, so many times.

The Last Train

The last train has gone into
the ether, looking for my father,
leaving a cloud of smoke.

The sky's the blue of his jacket,
his cap darker, the word *Guard*
in bright brass, shining among

the stars. Wherever I go, these
carriages take me, sitting
beside a man who never went

anywhere but to work and
to the Savannah with his goats.
Any dalliance or delay he kept

in a private pocket, along with
his whistle, each blast a warning
it was time to board. Time

to find the sleeper buried under
the house, and put it to stand
in the garden next to my mother's

fern, its fronds touching the spikes,
reaching for his phantom thumb, lost
someplace between here and Arouca.

The Last Island

Shaped like a boot, it hangs
like a pendant near the coast
of Venezuela, broken off

from the mainland like a piece
from a puzzle. Our rivers cross
the Bocas and flow backwards

till they reach our mountains.
Today, a refugee might ride
that current to find a village

and join the singing and
dancing, becoming a lead
among the *parranderos*.

I don't know how or when
my mother came, an infant,
she and her brother sent

to live among the Bajans
and locals all gathered there
in a common place, beyond it

nothing but open water,
The Atlantic swirling south,
not another rock to call home.

Cartagena

for Susana

She went to the old writer's town,
to that bistro, his favorite place
to meet and drink with the *campesinos,*
where girls would smooth his hair

while he told stories of sickness
cured by romance and of a dead girl
whose hair kept growing. There,
in a dark corner, under a portrait

of Gabo himself, she met a *guardia*
on leave from his country, who offered
to buy her something, anything.
But it's the writer who holds her interest.

She imagines him extending a hand
before leading her in a wild *paseo*,
she who hardly danced that she can
remember, introducing herself in mid-dip—

a poet, *sí*, her Spanish so alive, her
zapatos, her *corazón,* her *alma*!

Bluefields

Reminds me of the town I come from
in Trinidad, lanes and little houses.
This is a good road the Americans
left you, so we speed at the ninety
your wife warned me you like to do.
Perhaps your Jaguar demands it.
I wish I'd stayed in the other car,
the finger I closed the door on
still tingling, the little birds Hope
cooked still bitter on my tongue.
Tony's poem about defecating
on a neighbor's porch repeats its
scatology in my ear, the door of
every little house we pass open, like
this was the safest place in the world.

Lunch in Linstead

for Cmac

You'd warned me your mother
wasn't a great cook. She'd prepared
some birds caught by local boys.

They were bitter, the taste lingering
while Tony read us his latest poem.
I admired the patience with which

she listened. I pictured her
fussing over the birds' little bodies,
the way she nodded and smiled

as her son waited for a response, one
hand holding the page aloft, the other
picking at the bones on his plate.

Rundown

At Jenny's house, I ask the helper
how far she walks to get to work.
She describes the five-mile trek from
her home, the dark hour she sets out.

Sea salt is the trick, she tells me
as she sprinkles it on green bananas,
mackerel swimming in palm oil.
I dislike Jenny's husband's tone as

he orders her to fix my breakfast.
I take a picture as she glances out
the open window, the treetops like
green heads marching down the hill.

Nine Miles

In the village where Marley
was born, so-called because
it's nine miles from Alexandria,

a line of women in green, gold,
and red tams circle his tomb,
singing one of his songs.

The air is thick with incense smoke.
The mood is solemn until
a boy emerges from the bush,

offering us oranges. They look
green, but he swears they're sweet.
From a tinny player held to his ear,

I hear strains of "Soca Baptist,"
the hit calypso from Trinidad
Carnival this year.

One good thing about music,
the women sing, *when it hits you*
feel no pain …

Goshen

is the town in the hills
where we sat in the bar
as four men played *mento,*
the music that shares roots
with calypso. I was sick from

the pepper shrimp I had in Negril,
or it might have been the rum
we drank, shot after shot,
singing along to songs
we didn't know.

It was fun until the man
who said he was a mechanic
followed us outside, offering
to fix your car. Somehow
we managed to do it ourselves

and took off down the hill,
looking back as he stood, waving.
I recall that hand, streaked with dirt,
as he reached across the table
to pat yours, next to mine.

The Poet

They'll read your work in rooms
where the host describes you as
funny. They'll touch your hand,
and remind you to sign one for
the daughter they haven't seen

in years, who's out on the coast
somewhere, having a hard time
coming to terms with a mother
who seeks everyone's happiness
before her own. They'll pick up

a book and find the one line
of solace you offer among the
many distraught ones, about
a carpenter who fell in love
with a prostitute and built her

a dream house. And they'll
read it back to you, how he
smoothed the purple heart
wood into impossible rooms,
a gift you hardly recall giving.

A Blur

for Zadie

As a toddler, my granddaughter
had trouble with balance, wobbled
along a ledge while her therapist
held her hand. We lost every race

we ran with her brother, even
with the head start he gave us,
trailing into the building lobby
as he and the super high-fived

each other. Now her dad says
she came first in her high school
400m, third in the long jump. I'm
showing everyone the video, her

long legs a blur as I rewind and
point—that's her in the blue, no,
the other blue, her braid like
a bird in the air behind her,

like the arm that once held her
steady as she fought to put one
foot in front of the other, that foot
now crossing the finish line first.

Bureau of Sewers

The bus I take after seeing my friend
at the Four Seasons Nursing Home is
packed with schoolkids. On a building

we pass, the sign reads, *Bureau of Sewers.*
I picture what's inside—rows of desks,
clerks poring over plans of the city,

canals running out to sea. It's a windowless
structure, meant to encourage few visitors.
It makes me think of my friend, sleeping

stiffly upright as the nurse pushed him, only
his eyelids fluttering when I called his name,
the band on his arm warning, *Likely to fall.*

His head at an angle, he looked as if he were
listening to a bird trilling in a tree, the attendants
rubbing his shoulders each time they passed.

Next visit, I'll tell him about the Bureau,
and the noisy kids, and he'll remind me
how shit backs up, on given days.

Aripo Heights

for LeRoy

Today a girl's body was found
in a gully among dry leaves

where flowers bloom like nothing
happened. And the one-armed farmer

plants again, his attackers
driving by laughing at how he

holds the rope leading his cow.
He waves the stump at his artist neighbor,

who draws from his courage,
paints the wound on huge canvases,

leaves them to dry in the open
where the brassy smell of snakes

warns which path not to take
while killers pass with another soul

they tortured, flinging her remains off
the edge of our world, our common place.

The Man Writing in the Rain

His jacket is soaked, but he
keeps writing, bent over
a thick, black binder.

I wonder what the words say,
what compels him to sit by
The Hollows even after nightfall.

I stop near his bench sometimes,
pretending to tie my laces or
pick up a curious seed. But his eyes

never once lift from the page,
at which I glance in passing, his
words dark, and upside down.

When It's Night in Other Places

In the evening, I can almost smell the breeze
that blows across the Savannah, that comes
as darkness descends from up in the hills.

I can hear traffic slowing, the voices of old
men on the bench facing Cadiz Road,
sentences further and further apart, until

they grow quiet, each smiling to himself.
Each is rehearsing his own story, wondering
if it's worth breaking the silence for.

I know which one will get up first, who will
dust the seat of his pants, glance over the rails
at the candleflies winking and say, *I going in.*

I hold my breath as he stands at the curb
timing the cars, and the lights, for he's slow,
thinking of the window that's hard to close.

Three Chains

Beachfront property extends
to the high-water mark, no farther,
except in Tobago, where you're

granted an extra three chains.
So you may call it your private
beach where you gather,

have daiquiris by the gallon,
dip in your pool till your
fingers shrivel. But the sand,

down to the water's edge where
the foam retreats to become
wave again, is ours. We the people

can claim the island's perimeter,
sink our feet to the ankles in
sand dollar and shell, pretend we

own one of those yachts out there,
since like flotsam we arrived,
and like driftwood, we stayed.

ACKNOWLEDGEMENTS

The author wishes to express sincere gratitude to these publishers for their kindness in allowing the selected poems to appear in this publication, some in slightly revised form:

An Island of His Own (1992), *The Goat* (1999), and *Gone Away* (2006), Junction Press.
No Back Door (2010), *The Waving Gallery* (2014), *Voices Carry* (2017), and *Country of Warm Snow* (2020), Shearsman Books.
News of the Living (2020) and *The Last Train* (2023), Broadstone Books.

Gratitude also to the following publications where some of the poems initially appeared:
"After the Flood," "The Fight," Boston Review
"Status," "My Father's Jacket," upstreet
"Resistance," Killens Review of Arts & Letters
"Cataract," "Characters," Musings in a Tea Shop, edited by Gershia Mahabir

A huge debt of gratitude is owed to Susana Case for her close reading of these poems and her recommendations for changes where needed, as well as to Ihsan Taylor, whose editorial skills unfailingly find errant commas and intrusive spaces.

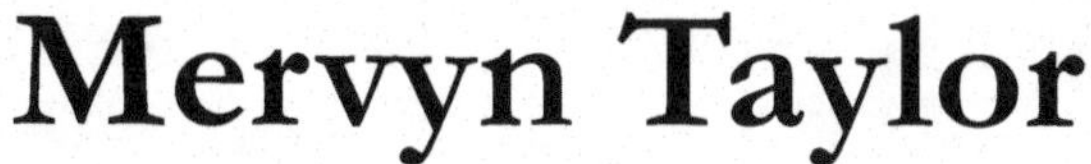

Mervyn Taylor

Mervyn Taylor, a Trinidad-born poet, is the author of eight full-length collections of poetry, including *No Back Door* (2010), *The Waving Gallery* (2014), and *Country of Warm Snow* (2020), a Poetry Book Society Recommendation that was listed for the Bocas Lit Prize. A chapbook, *News of the Living: Corona Poems*, was published by Broadstone in 2020. His latest full-length, also from Broadstone Books, is *The Last Train* (2023). Taylor has taught at Bronx Community College, The New School University, and in the NYC public school system. Besides poetry, he creates assemblage and Carnival art. His grandkids are Julian and Zadie, Sarai and Taj.

GETTING THROUGH

PRINTING WAS COMPLETED IN SEPTEMBER 2024 FOR **Beltway Editions**